THE PHILIPPINES

Your Ultimate Guide to Traveling, Culture, History, Food and More!

By Asha Miyazaki

EXPERIENCE EVERYTHING TRAVEL GUIDE COLLECTION™

EXPERIENCE EVERYTHING PUBLISHING

Forward

Thank you for purchasing this book from the Experience Everything Travel Guide Collection™! Inside you will find a ton of useful, informative and entertaining information on the Philippines and it is our desire that this book will provide you with the inspiration to explore!

Disclaimer

While this book contains a great deal of information, it does not have all of the information that is available on the Internet. It is written to inspire you about the destination rather than act as a full travel guide that you could use to get from point A to point B or to specific addresses/locations during your tour.

Contents:

See You In The Philippines!

Introduction

Tourists often visit the Philippines for its tropical climate, beaches, palm trees, rich history and exotic locale. However, it is the people that make the Philippines truly special.

Filipinos are very friendly, hospitable and kind people. If you wanted to be extra adventurous and actually live in the Philippines full time, they would welcome you and treat you like a local. In fact, a growing number of foreigners have been retiring and living in the country. The easy and laid-back lifestyle of the people has drawn the attention of the international community. The standard of living is also not that expensive making the Philippines a perfect place to live and visit.

The people in the country have a very positive attitude towards life. Imagine having been struck by the world's most powerful typhoon, Haiyan, in 2013. Filipinos still manage to smile and overcome the difficulties of life. Foreigners who wish to visit or live in the country will find it easy to adapt. You won't find it difficult to communicate as most of the people in the Philippines know how to speak English. Once you visit, you may never want to leave!

Chapter I: Geography

Islands, Islands, Islands!

The Philippines is an archipelago composed of 7,107 islands off Southeast Asia. The country lies between the Philippine Sea on the east and the South China Sea on the west. There are three major islands that make up the entire country. Luzon, the biggest, lies on the north, Visayas in the middle and Mindanao, the second largest, is found in the south. The country's closest neighbors include Taiwan, Malaysia, Indonesia, Vietnam and China.

The Philippines has a total of 298,000 square kilometers of land area and 2,000 square kilometers of water. That is why it isn't any wonder why the country is abundant in beaches. Some of these are not yet open for commercial purposes but can be visited with a prior booking. Although there are more than 7,000 islands in the country, the majority of its population inhabits only 11 of these islands.

Luzon Island and the Capital City, Manila

The biggest island in the country is Luzon where the capital city, Manila, is also located. It holds the center of business, trade and also has the most number of inhabitants. People who enjoy the hustle and bustle of city life will surely enjoy the sights and sounds Manila has to offer. Meanwhile, there are other places in Luzon that are not so fast paced.

As the country was colonialized by the Spaniards, many old houses and traces of wars lie in the different places in Luzon. Vigan City in Ilocos Sur holds majestic sights to these old, Spanish designed houses and a well-preserved European trade system. Visitors can take a 12 hour bus ride from Manila to Vigan, a UNESCO declared World Heritage Site.

Aside from Vigan, Luzon also holds the summer capital of the country. Baguio City is a seven hour bus ride from Manila. The city enjoys cool weather between 7 to 8 degrees Celsius and gets cooler during summertime in the country. Beach lovers can marvel the waters of Batangas, Pangasinan, Claveria, Sual, Zambales and Ibaan. Palawan is also a great place to visit for those who love to splash in the cool waters of the beach. In fact, the island was awarded the number one spot among the Top 30 Islands of the World during the Conde Nast Traveler Reader's Choice Award. Meanwhile, those who are in search of history and religion can visit Pampanga, Tarlac, Zambales, Batangas and Bataan while in Luzon.

Visayan Islands

The second island of the archipelago is the Visayan Islands which are divided into three regions. These are Region VI in the west, Region VII or referred to as Central Visayas and Region VIII found in the east.

Region VI is made up of six provinces including Aklan, Iloilo, Guimaras, Capiz, Antique and Negros Occidental. Region VII is made up of four provinces including Cebu, Bohol, Siquijor and Negros Oriental. Highly urbanized cities in the region include Lapu-Lapu City, Cebu City and Mandaue City. Meanwhile, Region VIII includes the provinces of Southern Leyte, Biliran, Eastern Samar, Northern Samar and Leyte and Samar.

The oldest city in the country, Cebu City, is found in central Visayas. It is the most urbanized and progressive city in the Visayan Island and is referred to as the Queen City of the South. The Chocolate Hills found in Bohol is also in this region. Region VI holds the famous Boracay Islands which ranked 12 in the Top 30 Islands of the World Award. The region is also home for world famous sweet mangoes found in the islands of Guimaras. Festivals also rock the Visayan Islands that are celebrated in different areas all year round. On the other hand, Region

VIII holds the longest bridge in the country, measuring 2,200 meters in length, that the provinces of Samar and Leyte.

Mindanao Island

The third major island in the Philippines is called Mindanao. It is also the second largest in terms of land area and is found down south of the country. Mindanao has 26 provinces grouped in six regions including Caraga, SOCCSARKGEN, Northern Mindanao, ARMM, Davao Region and the Zamboanga Peninsula.

Butuan City is the center of the Caraga Region. Meanwhile, other provinces include Surigao del Norte, Surigao del Sur, the Dinagat Island Province, Agusan del Norte and Agusan del Sur. Meanwhile, SOCCSARKGEN or Region XII is composed of the provinces of South Cotabato, Cotabato City, Cotabato, Sultan Kudarat and the Province of Sarangani. The center of the region is Koronadal City.

Northern Mindanao is composed of the provinces of Camiguin, Misamis Occidental and Oriental, Bukidnon and Lanao del Norte. The provinces of Sulu, Tawi-tawi, Maguindano, Lanao Del Sur and Basilan make up the entire Autonomous Region of Muslim Mindanao or ARMM.

The Davao Region is composed of Davao Oriental, Davao del Sur, Davao del Norte and the Compostela Valley. The last region of Mindanao, the Zamboanga Peninsula is made up of Isabela City, Zamboanga Sibugay, Zamboanga del Sur and Zamboanga del Norte.

Mindanao is known for its diversified culture and indigenous tribes. It also holds a huge number of Islam believers and is the eight most populous islands in the world. The island is also ranked as the 19th biggest island in the world having an area of 97,530 square kilometers.

The highest mountain in the country, Mt. Apo, is also found in Mindanao as well as the Marianas Trench, one of the greatest depths to exist measuring 10,800 meters deep, is found a few miles of the shore Mindanao. It is also the home of Lake Lanao, an ancient lake included in the 15 ancient lakes of the world, and the famous waterfalls Maria Cristina and Limunsudan.

Local and foreign surfers find Siargao a surfing haven. It is also the surfing capital of the Philippines where local and international competitions have already been held. Pristine beaches are also flourishing in Mindanao which includes the Pebble beach in Surigao del Norte, Zamboanga's Pink Beach of Santa Cruz and the Alano Beach in Basilan to name a few.

The Philippines is also a paradise for scuba divers and only a few countries can compete with the wide scuba destination it offers. Philippine scuba diving destinations offer a wide range of activities from diving and swimming with small, big and exotic fishes to shipwrecks during the World War II.

Weather

The Philippines enjoy two seasons: the wet and dry. Those who love the warm, tropical climate will be in heaven while in the country. The usual temperature in the country is between 25 to 28 degrees Celsius but can get really hot during summer.

Industry

The two main sources of livelihood in the country are agriculture and fishing. This is no surprise since plants thrive abundantly given the kind of climate the country has. With vast waters surrounding the Philippines, fishing has also become a primary source of livelihood to the locals. People who visit the country will be amazed to choose and eat from a wide variety of local seafood.

Chapter II: History of the Philippines

Discovery

The Philippines was discovered by explorer Ferdinand Magellan who sailed under the Spanish flag. Magellan was supposedly going to Spice Islands in Indonesia when he reached the Homonhon island of the Philippines on March 16, 1521. He was not able to explore the entire country as he was killed by a local named Lapu-Lapu during the battle in Mactan, Cebu.

In 1543, another expedition was sent by the Spanish King Philip II headed by Ruy Lopez de Villalobos wherein he named the country Las Islas Filipnas after the Spanish ruler. However, Spain's invasion did not start until another ship was sent in 1565 headed by Miguel Lopez de Legazpi. He set up Manila as the country's capital following a defeat from a Muslim ruler in Cebu six years after he first landed in the islands.

Colonization

The Spanish colonial times was full of bloodshed as Filipinos despised foreign invasion. This led to brilliant minds including the country's National Hero Dr. Jose P. Rizal to start a bloodless battle for freedom using his pen. He was able to write and publish novels such as the Noli Me Tangere and El Filibusterismo which angered the Spanish authorities. He showcased the cruelty of the Spaniards towards his fellowmen and the real scenario of the country under their leadership.

Rizal was sentenced to death in 1896 for treason after inspiring movements for freedom such as the Katipunan, a secret society headed by Andres Bonifacio and Magdalo headed by Emilio Aguinaldo. However, Bonifacio and Aguinaldo's pact did not agree on most terms resulting the murder of the former by the latter's soldiers. This caused Aguinaldo and his troops to be exiled in Hong Kong.

Meanwhile, when the war between Spain and the United States broke out in 1898 wherein the US won battle in Manila Bay, Aguinaldo was invited back to the Philippines. The American troops were already in the country when Aguinaldo reached shore. In June 12, 1898, the Philippines was able to declare independence from Spain and General Emilio Aguinaldo raised and waved the Philippine Flag for the first time in Kawit, Cavite.

From then, the Philippines has been a hot item to a number of invading countries. This included Japan who started occupying the country few hours after they bombed Pearl Harbor during the height of World War II. Japan occupied the Philippines for more than three years. The Philippines remained loyal to the United States because of the guarantee of independence following US General Douglas McArthur promise to come back and help free the country from the clutches of the Japanese. The general was true to his words when he came back on October 20, 1944 bringing war fleets and men. The fighting continued until the formal surrender of the Japanese troops on September 2, 1945.

Independence

A treaty was signed between the Philippines and the United States ratifying the June 12 independence day of the country to July 4, 1946. In April 23, 1946, Manuel Roxas was elected President of the Republic of the Philippines but died two years after due to a fatal heart attack. Elpidio Quirino assumed the post on April 17, 1948 which lasted for a year. Jose P. Laurel ran against Quirino a year after but was defeated in what he called was victory due to force. In 1953, a new president was elected into office in the person of Ramon Magsaysay who proudly wore the Barong Tagalog for the first time, the national costume for men. However, Magsaysay died after his plane crashed and was replaced by Vice President Carlos P. Garcia.

Garcia ran for presidency in the 1961 elections but was defeated by Diosdado Macapagal. In 1965, Macapagal decided to run for re-election but was defeated by Ferdinand Marcos. Marcos had the Philippines under Martial law from 1972 until 1981. His term ended in 1986 when Corazon Aquino, the first lady president of the country was elected into office. This was after her husband and presidential candidate bet against Marcos, Benigno Aquino Sr. was shot dead which ignited the iconic People Power movement.

After Aquino's term, General Fidel Ramos was elected into office in 1992 until the end of his term in 1998. He was then succeeded by Joseph Estrada whose term was cut short when another people power movement was held making Gloria Macapagal-Arroyo assumed office in 2001. After which, she ran again for office until her term ended in 2010. Benigno Aquino Jr., the son of Benigno Sr. And late President Aquino, is the current president of the country. His term ends in 2016 which will be followed by another presidential election.

Chapter III: Culture

The Philippines is not only a magnificent country to visit for its famous beaches and tourist spots, it is also filled with a rich history and a diversified culture. In fact, there are numerous ethnic tribes that composed the different major islands of the country. These groups also have their own language which cannot be understood when you travel from one place to another within the country. But that is not a big problem because there is one language that binds the people even as they come from different regions in the country.

Language

The Filipino language or Tagalog is widely spoken in the Luzon area. It is also the national language in the country. Filipinos don't have to worry if they're all the way from Mindanao because they are able to communicate with the people in Manila even though the dialect is different. As long as they know how to speak Tagalog, they will be able to effectively communicate with one another. The vast majority of Filipinos also know English and even if you run into a Filipino who can't speak English, there is usually someone around who can speak English well enough to translate the conversation.

Ethnicity

The ethnic group Bicolanos originated from Bicol, Luzon. There are 3.5 million speakers of Bicolano including those from the provinces of Naga, Daet, Legazpi, Sorsogon, Masbate and Albay. The Gaddangs, on the other hand, are people coming from the Cagayan Valley region, Nueva Vizcaya and Isabela while the Ibanags are from Isabela and Cagayan. Meanwhile, there are about 8 million speakers of the Ilokano dialect coming from the provinces of northern and central Luzon, Metro Manila and in some towns in the Visayas and Mindanao regions.

The northern part of Luzon are inhabited by the Ivatans who are linked with Taiwanese aborigines. The Kapampangans are people coming from the central plains of Luzon including Nueva Ecija and Bataan. Their language is also spoken by about 2 million people in the country. The Pangasinenses are the ninth largest ethnical group in the Philippines. They are primarily found in the seaboard of northwestern Luzon with residents in the Pangasinan province.

Meanwhile, the Visayan islands also hold a number of ethnic groups with their specific dialects. These include Ilonggo, Waray, Cebuano, Aklanon and Masbatenyo. Some people in the areas of Luzon and Mindanao also speak the dialects of those coming from the provinces of Visayas.

In Mindanao, the biggest Islam ethnic group in the country are the Moros comprising of the Maranaos, Tausug, Maguindanao, Yakan, Sama and the Banguingui. They make up around 5% to 10% of the population in the country. They also have their own system of justice and education based in Cotabato City, Mindanao. Meanwhile, the Subanon are the biggest non-Muslim ethnic group in Mindanao. They are often found in the provinces of Zamboanga, Misamis Oriental and Misamis Occidental and Basilan. The Chavacanos are settlers found in Zamboanga City, Sulu, Ternate, Davao, Tawi-Tawi and Davao. Their dialect is comparable to Spanish.

Religion and Way of Life

Filipino culture are known to be positive and very lively. When the country was devastated by Typhoon Haiyan in 2013, CNN cited the resiliency of the people to be able to smile despite the horrendous lash of the ravaging super typhoon. They are also known to uphold moral values that are already forgotten in other countries. For instance, a Filipino family will eat their meals together especially during dinner. A prayer is said before eating and the head of the family always gets the first share of the meal. Family time including going to church regardless of religion is also highly regarded.

There are two types of marriages prevailing in the country. These are the civil and the religious ceremonies. During a civil union, a mayor, judge or an eligible servant of law can conduct the marriage rites. Meanwhile, the religious ceremony for a wedding is officiated by a priest or a pastor depending on which sect the marrying couple belongs.

In recent times, arranged marriages are no longer observed in most families in the Philippines although some affluent families still practice the tradition. Most Filipinos wait until they are in their mid-twenties before settling down. It is a kind of pre-requisite to finish school and get a job to be able to ask a lady's hand for marriage. However, those who are stricken with poverty marry earlier than the ideal marrying age in the country.

Filipino families enjoy a huge number of children which can be up to a dozen. However, the growing prices of commodities have resulted to most families having one or two children or three at maximum. Filipinos also love kinship. That is why it is not a wonder when you see grandparents living in the same house with their grandchildren or even their great grandchildren. The houses of aunts, uncles and cousins are also closely built to each other.

The extended family relationships is very important to most Filipinos especially to their women. Mothers and daughters share decision making within the family. Marriages are also done in the hometown of the woman in case the bride and groom come from different provinces. Childcare is even shared especially when parents have to work. Rearing children is a shared responsibility of parents and grandparents. Education is highly regarded making it important to finish college from a reputable institution to be able to land a good job.

Religion also plays a big role in the Filipino culture. This must have been from the time when the Spaniards colonized the country and indoctrinated Catholicism. In fact, a majority of Filipinos are Catholics followed by other religious sectors. There are also a lot of old Catholic churches in the country and a large number of devotees.

Music and Entertainment

Music has also become a big player in the Filipino culture. In fact, their music has also evolved with time. Although Filipinos have their own local songs and musical instruments, the influence of the western countries has already become viral. This includes listening to the like of Jazz, Rhythm and Blues, Rock and Slow Rock, English Love Songs and even Hip-Hop.

The Filipino youth nowadays have been reached with the hip-hop music culture both in the local scene and in the United States. This paved way for the inception of FlipTop League Battle, where in battle emcees display their wits in a modern day debate of rapping and free style verses. This has attracted the youth coming from the different parts of the country to join and showcase their talents. Some of their emcees including Anygma and Protege have even traveled to Canada for rap battle league competitions.

Filipinos are also known to be fans of TV series. Don't be surprised to see an entire family glued to a TV screen at primetime waiting for their favorite soap to air. In the rural areas, listening to the radio are a family's way of recreation.

Celebrations

Festivals and events are also a part of the Filipino culture. Fiestas are mostly celebrated in honor of a town's religious patron saint. Events such as these celebrated in the provinces are to watch for. A roasted whole pig brushed with Filipino spices will surely entice meat lovers as this is mostly present during festivities. Aside from this, events that showcases the talents of Filipinos are also widely celebrated in the different areas of the country. Indeed the Filipino spirit towards merry making is full of passion as displayed in their culture!

Chapter IV: Getting Around

Getting around the places in the country does not require huge sums of cash. You can travel roundtrip by plane to reach another part of the archipelago for US$100 at maximum. Aside from that, the cost of transportation is reasonable for its distance.

Popular means of transportation in the Philippines include, jeepneys, ferries, taxis, pedicubs, rail systems, bancas, tricycles, buses, planes and the habal-habals.

Jeepneys

The idea of jeepneys came after World War II. Filipino entrepreneurs thought about it as a possible mode of transportation by turning jeeps into colorful and longer vehicles in areas that cannot accommodate buses. There are several types of jeepneys including the 10-seater and the 14-seater. They are also referred to as the kings of the roads in the country given their number and the wider routes they cover within an area. Currently, the standard jeepney fare is P8.00 with discounts for the elderly, PWD and students. The fare increases as the distance also increase.

Jeepneys have been very popular to tourists and riding one is a must. It has been an icon in the Philippine streets and almost everyone has rode a jeepney to work, school, going to the mall or simply having a joy ride.

Riding a jeepney is simple. Stand beside the loading/unloading stop for jeepneys. Wave your hand as if calling a jeepney to come over. You will be able to see the name of the location where you will be heading to or areas within your destination written on placards. This will help passengers identify the right jeep for the right route to take.

To pay for a ride, one must say, "bayad po" and hand over the fare to the person in front which will be passed to the driver if a jeepney conductor, the guy who gets the fare and the one calling on to the driver to go or stop, is not present. "Para po" means you want to go down from the jeep or you have already reached your destination.

If you are not sure about the place you are going, you can always ask the driver. They will be glad to tell you the right jeepney to take or if the distance is too far, they would advise you take a cab or the bus instead. Meanwhile, if you are not sure where to go down, you can also advise the driver to stop at the nearest place where you will be able to take another jeepney or walk towards where you are going.

When inside the jeepney, it is always advised to be mindful of your personal belongings. Remember not to let your expensive things out as this can attract thieves or robbers who might also be taking the same jeepney ride with the rest of the passengers.

Buses

Philippine transportation for long distance travel suggests that you take the bus. You can either take the non-airconditioned bus, which is a lot cheaper, or the airconditioned one. If you happen to take the non-airconditioned bus, take note of the heat that you would experience along the way as most of these buses are jampacked.

Buses operating from Manila to provinces are privately owned. They usually go from the capital to major centrals of the provinces, vice versa. They connect far distanced places which makes it a lot convenient for travelers. The schedules vary so if you happen to plan a trip out of the city, be sure to check bus details from their offices or online.

The fare depends on the distance of the place where you are going. Typically it can start from P100 up. Buses have fare tariffs so you won't have to worry about getting over charged for a trip. The route of the bus is also displayed on placards similar to jeepneys. The bus conductor receives your fare while some operators have tickets sold in their booths within the bus stations. You don't have to worry about getting lost as the conductor announces the name of the place where the bus stops. At the end of the trip, he will tell passengers when it's already time to alight the bus.

Tricycles

Tricycles are modified motorcycles used as a kind of taxi in the Philippines. The design varies from one place to another although they still serve a common purpose: to get you where you want to go. These tricycles are similar to the auto rickshaws found in India and Thailand's tuk-tuks.

A tricycle cab is attached to one side of the motorcycle where passengers can sit. Passengers can also choose to sit behind the driver. Subdivisions and some streets make use of tricycle transportation. It is a convenient ride to take when going to the local market or other short distance travels. However, city restrictions often disallow tricycles to operate in main streets because they can contribute to traffic. The tricycle fare starts from P8 pesos and can go up to as much as P50 especially when you ride it alone and have it take you to your destination without other passengers on board.

Pedicabs

Another mode of transportation in the Philippines is the pedicab. It is a three-wheel bicycle with a covered cab and seat. It usually operates inside subdivisions or short distance places. The pedicab has various names depending on the regions where it operates. For instance, Ilonggos call them "trisikad" while those in Manila call them "padyak".

Two people can ride the pedicab when going to places with narrow streets. However, these mode of transportation cannot go beyond areas where much traffic is anticipated. The fare starts from P7 to as much as P30 pesos depending on where you wish to go.

Light Rail Transit System (LRT)

The Metro Manila Light Rail Transit System or the LRT offers passengers faster way to access far and traffic routes like Baclaran, EDSA and Monumento. The major reason for the establishment of these transportation system was to decongest the heavy traffic in the Metro. Currently, there are 29 LRT stations that you can conveniently choose to be near the place where you are supposed to go.

In 1999, Taft Avenue in Pasay City was made nearer to Quezon City's North Avenue as the Metro Rail Trail System or MRT was made open to the public. Currently, the MRT has 13 stations.

The fare is also cheap considering the far distances of one station to another. It starts from P15 per train ticket, available in the station, depending on the station where you want to alight. Passengers can also avail of the "store valued ticket" payable one time. This will allow you to go inside the train right away without having the burden of lining up to purchase a single trip ticket.

Every day, about 2.1 million people take the LRT. If you want to try it, be sure not to ride during peak hours that start from 7:00 AM until about 9:00 AM. Lunchtime is also included in the peak hours as well as from 5:00 PM to 7:00 PM. The train has no smoking area and strictly no pets allowed. The train starts operating at 6:00 AM and ends at 9:00 PM. Be sure to get a ride before 9:00 PM if you are planning to take a train ride home.

Taxi Cabs

Another mode of transportation is by taking a taxi cab available in city areas. Metered taxis are flourishing in every city in the Philippines so you won't have to worry about getting one home. However, you have to take note that taxis are scarce especially during peak hours and rainy days.

The flag down of a taxi cab starts at P40 and increases P2.50 for every 250 meters. However, a new rule has been set out to minus P10 from the total fare you have to pay from a taxi ride which you have to remind the cab driver in case he forgets to subtract.

Remember to keep the doors locked and the windows up when taking a taxi ride to avoid unwanted situations such as robbery. Check if the meter is turned on to ensure that you only pay for the accumulated distance of the trip incurred. There are also different breeds of taxi drivers whom you have to watch out for. They can rip you off your pockets if you bag their call for very expensive fares even for a not so far trip. There are help desks located in the airports in case you are doubtful about the cost of the trip you are being charged for.

Ferries

Meanwhile, ferries and inter-island vessels operate between major island travels. If you are not in a hurry, you can take a boat ride to the next region located in Luzon, Visayas or Mindanao. The fare also varies so it would be best to call the shipping lines first or view their price list online.

Planes

If you want to travel a lot faster to your next destination, take a plane ride going to major islands in the country. The Philippines have three major airplanes. The Philippine Airlines, the country's flag carrier, Cebu Pacific and Air Asia. They have wide list of destinations which are traveled from as short as 25 minutes to as long as a 3 hour trip depending from where port of origin is.

Bancas (Boats)

As the Philippines is composed of more than seven thousand islands, it would be impossible to tour around these without having to use a banca, a small boat made of wood sometime equipped with a motor engine for faster travel. A boat man will serve as the captain of the banca with one or two assistants on board. The fare ride depends on the distance of the port to the destination. Some passengers pay the fare that would sum up the entire trip should they wish to have an exclusive trip using the banca.

Habal-Habals (Motorcycles)

Lastly, the habal-habal is an improvised motorcycle ride with a flat wood attached on the seat behind the driver. Unbelievable, it can carry more than its passenger capacity without having to struggle with difficulty. The habal-habal is found mostly in rural areas and used as a mode of transportation when going up mountainous places. It is also abundant in places in the Mindanao island.

Chapter V: Where to Stay

The Philippine Islands is a growing tourist destination. It receives a hefty number of visitors annually according to the data provided by the Department of Tourism. In 2013, the country has attracted more than 4 million tourists with South Koreans at 1.17 million, the largest group of visitors to enter Philippines at the time.

Aside from South Korean visitors, those coming from Canada, the United States, China, Japan, Taiwan and Australia also enjoy the Philippine Islands. In 2014, a total of 4,333,368 tourists visited the country.

Manila

There are a lot of hotels for travelers who wish to visit the Philippines. The abundance of the tourism industry has paved the way for luxurious, world class hotels to rise in the country. In Manila, the Pan Pacific Manila Hotel is the first luxury hotel located in Malate.

Affluent travelers often choose this hotel due to its royal treatment through its butler service. Other famous luxury hotels the capital include the Makati Shangri-la Manila, Sofitel Philippine Plaza, InterContinental Manila, Fairmont, Dusit Thani, Hotel Jen, Raffles Hotel and Hotel H2o Manila. Take note that the prices of these hotels are quite expensive. Should you wish to settle for budget hotels and inns while in Manila, there are also a number of choices to choose from.

The Fort Budget Inn in Bonifacio Global City located in Taguig, Metro Manila is often times considered by travelers. White Knight Hotel is also a good choice when visiting Intramuros, Manila. Other choices include the Manila Venetian Hotel, Malate Pensionne, Binondo Suites, Riviera Mansion Hotel, BP International Hotel, Lotus Garden Hotel and the Bayview Park Hotel. These hotels are budget friendly and offer great customer service located all around Manila.

Meanwhile, if you are roaming the majestic beaches of Palawan Island, Amanpulo and Pangulasian Island Resort are the best choices for luxury service. For mid-range hotel prices while in Palawan, you can book a stay with Palawan Village Hotel, Coron Westown Resort, Sophia's Garden Resort, El Nido Cove Resort, El Rio y Mar Resort or Go Hotels Puerto Princesa.

Visayan Islands

There are also numerous luxury hotels when visiting the Visayan Islands. If you happen to be in Cebu, Shangri-la Mactan is a good choice. Imperial Palace Resort and Spa is also a popular luxury hotel in Cebu. Meanwhile, other luxury hotels in Cebu include Abaca Beach Resort, Maribago Bluewaters, Marco Polo Plaza Cebu, Alegre Beach Resort, Sumilon Island Resort and the Marriot Hotel Cebu.

For cheaper accommodation but still great customer service, Westpoint Inn, GV Tower Hotel, Express Inn, Robe's Pension House, Cebuview Tourist Inn and Travelbee Capitol Inn are great choices while in Cebu.

Boracay

Boracay is also a popular destination for tourists due to its cool waters, white sandy shores and relaxing ambiance. Hotels have also flourished in the island following the demand from tourists coming from all over the world.

Prior to reaching the Boracay Island, some people go around nearby cities including Iloilo. There are numerous places to stay in Iloilo City including first class hotels and comfort inns that would best fit your budget. Sarabia Hotel, Hotel del Rio, Days Hotel and Amigo Terrace Hotel are the big players in Iloilo City. Other hotels include The Grand

Hotel, Circle Inn, Westtown Hotel, Diversion 21, Casa La Granja and Go Hotels Iloilo. There are also a number of pensions houses that you can choose from. If you are unsure of where to stay, friendly taxi drivers in the city are the best people to ask from. You can also come to the city's tourism department or have it checked online.

After you have marveled Iloilo City, you can go to Boracay island by taking a 4 to 5 hour bus ride. The island is divide into 3 stations. Each of these stations have numerous hotels to choose from. This includes Discovery Shores Boracay, The Villa, Fridays Boracay, Ambassador in Paradise, One Azul, Boracay Terraces and the Royal Park Hotel Boracay. All of these hotels are found in the not so crowded station 1.

Station 2 also offers a lot of hotels as this the restaurant, shopping and entertainment capital of the island. Hotels include Boracay Regency, The District Boracay, La Carmela de Boracay, The Tides Boracay, Hennan Garden Resort, Boracay Tropics Resort Hotel and the Crown Regency Resort and Convention Center.

Meanwhile, Station 3 holds budget inns and bungalows although upscale hotels have been developing in this part of the island. The Asya Premier Suites, Mandala Spa and Villas, Paradise Garden Hotel, The Rose Pike, Hey Jude South Beach Hotel, Dive Gurus Boracay Beach, Erus Suites Boracay, Arwana Boracay and the Island Jewel Inn are located in this area.

Davao City

On the other hand, travelers visiting Mindanao often flock Davao City and the nearby provinces. This is because it is more peaceful in the area after the government launched an attack to rebels situated in various locations in Mindanao.

Davao holds different hotels varying from service and prices. This includes the Marco Polo Davao, Bahay ni Tuding Inn, Green Windows Dormitel, Tune Hotel, Hotel Tropika, Seda Abreeza Davao, Hotel

Galleria Davao, Park Inn by Radisson, Waterfront Insular Davao and the Big Apple Hotel. Other choices also include the Red Knight Gardens, My Hotel, Tinhat Boutique Hotel & Restaurant, Eden Nature Park & Resort, Microtel Inn by Windham and the Casa Leticia Boutique Hotel.

When in the Philippines, places to stay that best fit the budget is not a problem. The country offers a wide variety of hotel, inns, pension houses, hostels, dormitels and even condominiums for transient boarding. Most of the prices range from as high as US$500/day to as low $20/night. The best thing to do prior your visit is have a browse online for various hotels to stay in the destination where you are heading.

Remember that the country holds more than 7,000 islands to discover and having a prior booking always helps to ease hotel stresses. A good recommendation from friends or relatives who have already visited the country would be a great help. Traveler magazines also offer suggestions for places to stay in the Philippines. Online hotel reviews are also a good way to get you started before making your booking decision.

Chapter VI: Where to Go and What to Eat

The must see places in the country are situated throughout the entire Philippines. You can't just visit one place in Luzon as you would miss out the fun in the Visayas and Mindanao islands. A 5 day vacation won't be enough to be able to discover the wonders of the country. However, if your vacation is tight with the schedules, the country offers nearby destinations that would satisfy short period of trips.

Tourists coming from various parts of the world often land in the Ninoy International Airport, Manila. The capital holds the biggest airport in the country where international flights mostly operate although Iloilo, Negros Occidental, Cebu and Davao also receive international flights in their respective airports.

Manila

There are a number of nearby destinations if you happen to choose Manila as your nearest gateway to the Philippines. Start by going to Intramuros, the historic center of Manila, and take the classic kalesa ride for P350. If you don't want to go for a horse ride, walking around Intramuros would also mark a great experience especially for those who want a taste of rich history.

The entire city is dubbed as the city within the city filled with defensive walls. It once served as a defense ground for the colonial government during the Spanish regime. You can also go up to the Buluarte de Dilao. It is the best spot to watch people coming from all walks of life taking a stroll around Intramuros.

The city also has a lot of plazas and other attractions that won't require you any payment. It is best to take pictures and walk along its cobbled streets. You can do this without hiring expensive tour guides to assist you. If you decide to visit Intramuros, be sure to go before 10 AM while the heat of the sun is still tolerable. You can enjoy a sweet ensaymada paired with Spanish hot choco in this colonial heritage from the Spanish era.

For those who dig art, Manila's contemporary art works are found along Chino Roces Avenue. Manila Contemporary has hosted art exhibits from local to international artists. Silverlens also lies nearby for those who love photography and installation and video works. While in the metro, don't forget to drop by Cafe Juanita in Pasig for delicious home cooked Filipino dishes. The aligue (crab fat) is a must try dish along with the laing (taro leaves with coconut milk sauce) and the asohos (whitting), deep fried to perfection.

If you're up to shop, Greenbelt 3 showcases wide choices for your shopping spree while in Manila. As we know, Philippines is a predominantly Catholic country and even in the center of the shopping arena lies the Greenbelt Chapel, placed in the center of the meticulously landscaped garden.

Museums are also abundant in the metro including those showcasing rich families' works of art. You can check out the Ayala Museum in Makati and the Yuchengco Musuem along Gil Puyat Avenue.

While roaming the busy streets of Manila, don't forget to get yourself a bowl of halo-halo. This popular Filipino dessert resembles the combined cultures, wide heritage and the rich history of the country. The dessert is made with shaved iced, sweetened beans, fruits, Filipino creamed caramel (leche flan), ube , nata de coco and milk. Top it off with a scoop of ube flavor ice cream to complete the cool, refreshing taste of the halo-halo.

Another area to visit while in the city is the chinatown of Manila, Binondo. In here you will find a rich culture that has greatly influenced the Filipino way of life. Binondo holds a lot of stores offering merchandise that are cheaper compared to those you find in the mall. Binondo also holds a number of Chinese specialty restaurants that serves authentic Chinese flavors. Exotic foods are also found in this area including the infamous Soup No. 5.

Soup No. 5 is actually cow penis boiled in broth and mixed with other beef cut into cubes. Technically, you don't know it's inside the bowl. You would be surprised to know after devouring one soup bowl that it's actually there. Try it in Cafe Mezzanine Binondo or in El Mondo Restaurant.

The nightlife in Manila is also lively and hip. Numerous bars with both local and international DJs mixing the beat are a must see when spending the night out. Good choices to go include the Hobbit House in Ermita, Che'lu Bar, Cowboy Grill and Exklusiv in Malate, 71 Gramercy and Bond Urban Pub in Makati. If you're down for some hip hop and rhyme battles, BSide at Collective in Makati is also a popular choice.

Tagaytay City in Cavite

The nearest place you can divert your tour to is Tagaytay City in Cavite. This is a 2 hour drive from the metro and is situated in the highlands. Grab a jacket as the temperature here is cooler compared to Manila.

Activities including picnic, zipline and horseback riding is popular among guests visiting the highlands. A visit in Tagaytay will not be complete without catching the sight of the Taal Volcano and the Taal Lake. Restaurants are also flourishing located along Aguinaldo Highway where you can still catch the view of the splendid sights. Don't forget to try the Bulalo, made from beef shanks and marrow, for lunch!

Albay

After a tour in the metro, you might want to hop in a bus and go to Albay. The Bicol region is a 12 hour bus ride from the capital. Although the ride is quite long, you are assured of a worthy long sit experiencing.

The first thing to do while in Albay is visit the Mayon Volcano. The almost perfect cone of the volcano will surely get you enthralled. You can pay a local registered guide (expensive) to take you for a hike towards the crater. You can also get close to the volcano by driving along the scenic roads of the Mayon Skyline.

While in Albay, take a feast in the local cuisine including the Bicol Express. Warning! This is not for the faint hearted. The overly spicy taste of Bicol Express (pork meat in chili and coconut sauce) can get you asking for more glasses of water. Try the pancit rinuguan if you are feeling a little bit of adventurous over a meal. This is made up of noodles in pork blood and innards' broth.

Cebu

Going down in the Visayan Islands, a must visit place is Cebu. It is a highly competitive, urbanized district with big shopping malls, historic scenes and marvelous nightlife experience. The Penthouse in the city district is a must visit place for clubbing. Other party places in Cebu include LoneStar Saloon Bar, Amnezia Superclub, Marshall's Irish Pub, The Den and Pipeline.

Aside from partying, Cebu also offers magnificent heritage sites including the Magellan's Cross. This is an iconic symbol when the Portugese explorer Ferdinand Magellan landed in the island and propagated the ideals of Catholicism in the islands and beyond. You can also checkout the smallest fort in the country located in Cebu City, Fort San Pedro. The Mactan Shrine is another tourist destination showing a life size monument of the local chief who defeated Magellan in a battle.

If you are feeling a little fishy, dig in Tabo-an Market for great deals of dried squid and other local fish. Crown Regency Hotel in Fuente

Osmena also offer the Sky Adventure allowing guests to experience heart pounding tower walks and the urban zipline. Cebu also boasts its famous Lechon de Cebu (roasted pork) and the "puso" (rice wrapped in palm leaves). Travelers should feast on these as they are only available in this particular region.

Davao

Tourists going down Mindanao should visit Davao. This is a major city of the island where most happenings, nightlife and good food flourish although great dishes are served all throughout Mindanao. Davao is the home of the Philippine Eagle, the country's national bird. However, it's just more than birds that people come here. The magnificent view, historic sites, great beaches and the food are what's keeping people coming to and fro.

Relax and unwind in Matina Shrine Hills where Jack's Ridge, a Japanese headquarters during the World War II, is located. Jack's Ridge offers dining experience and many recreational activities. You can a taxi ride going to Jack's Ridge that would cost about P150. You can also take a jeepney ride that will cost from P10 to P15. From then, a tricycle should be able to take you to the location.

Located about an hour from the city, the Philippine Eagle Center is the center for the infamous Philippine Eagles. You will be charged P50 for the entrance fees while those below 18 years old should pay P30. If you want to get close with nature, the Malagos Garden Resort is located nearby. The wildlife garden's attraction includes a bird park, butterfly sanctuary and a zoo.

The nightlife in Davao City is also as vibrant as in Cebu and Manila. However, you have to be mindful as the entire city is a non-smoking zone especially in public places. Famous party places include Damosa Gateway, Prime Square, Habana Compound, Paseo de Legazpi and Bistro Cellar de Oboza.

A Davao tour will not be completed without a taste of its mouthwatering dishes. The city is famous for its kinilaw na tuna (raw tuna fish in vinegar), Sinuglaw (a grilled pork belly and kinilaw combo), Sinugbang Nokus (grilled squid), Guso (fresh seaweed salad) and the Dinuguan (pork innards with blood for broth).

Philippine exotic foods can be mostly found throughout the streets in the country. Your Philippine tour experience will not be complete without having "balot" after dinner or eating "isaw", "betamax" and "adidas". Balot is actually steamed duck egg with its embryo inside while isaw, chicken intestine, betamax, pork blood and adidas, chicken feet are best eaten when grilled. Don't forget to get hold of your adobo meal, (pork cubes in vinegar and soy sauce) as this is the national dish of the country and is served in Filipino restaurants and almost every home.

Chapter VII: Must See Festivals and Events

As the Filipino is rich in culture and heritage, it won't come as a surprise if almost every month, festivals and events are happening throughout the country.

January

In January, the year kicks off with the Feast of the Black Nazarene in Quiapo, Manila. Thousands of devotees march with the Black Nazarene on the streets from the Quiapo Church, vice versa. This is an intense event for most Catholics who do this annually to strengthen their devotion. Recently, Pope Francis visited Manila where numerous devotees both local and foreign went to march in the streets and attend the Catholic gathering.

After the much celebrated religious festivities in Manila, Aklan holds its Ati-Ati Festival during the third week of January. The festival is in commemoration of the land deal between the chieftains of Borneo with aborigines of Aklan. People can dance in the streets to the beat of the drum and lyre along with dancers dressed in Aeta costumes. Sinulog Festival in Cebu is simultaneously celebrated with the Ati-Atihan fest in Kalibo, Aklan. The festival is celebrated on the fourth Sunday of January in honor of the image of the Sto. Nino, a catholic belief. Street dancing, drum beats, good food and nightlife dominates the entire center of Cebu.

January is finally ended with the Dinagyang Festival celebrated in Iloilo City. The celebration is also in honor of the child Jesus, Sto. Nino. It showcases different contestants painted in black and dressed in aboriginal costumes while dancing to the beat of the drums. Tourists can enjoy watching competing tribes under the heat of the sun.

February

February starts with the Feast of the Lady of Candles in Jaro, Iloilo City. This is a big, religious festival celebrated in February 2 which usually have roads closed and classes suspended due to heavy traffic. Meanwhile, February 12 to 15 is the celebration of the Hot Air Festival in Pampanga. Awesome hot air balloons fly as the sun rises in Clark, Pampanga. February 28 marks the Panagbenga Festival in Baguio. This is where different varieties of flowers are arranged in trucks that go on parade.

March

March is the ultimate month for the music festival in Puerto Galera as they celebrate the Malasimbo Music & Arts Festival. Bukidnon in Mindanao also holds their festivity as they celebrate the Kaamulan Festival, a festival of the 7 ethnic tribes in the region., celebrated from March 7 to 8.

April

When the Holy Week for Catholics fall on April, different programs showing the life of Jesus Christ is dramatized until his crucifixion. Before, men who pledges to act as Christ are nailed to the cross until the Catholic church banned the practice.

May

In May, Pahiyas Festival is celebrated in Lucban, Quezon to commemorate good harvest and the bountiful times of their people. This is celebrated every 15th day of May. Meanwhile, the Feast in Obando is a must visit for couples who are trying to conceive a child. The fertility rites is celebrated from May 17 to 19 where men and women dance in the streets in prayer of marriage or to have a child.

June

June 12 is the National Independence Day of the Philippines from the Spaniards. This is an official holiday where work and classes are not observed. The ceremonial rites include giving a wreath of flowers to the national hero Dr. Jose Rizal's statue iby the Philippine President n Luneta Park. Meanwhile, June 24 is the Feast of the Lechon in Balayan, Batangas. You will see a number of roasted pigs parading the streets and are eaten by spectators afterwards.

July

From July 25 to 26, Tagbilaran, Bohol celebrates the Sandugo Festival remembering the treaty of friendship of the local chief Datu Sikatuna with the Spanish King's representative Miguel Lopez de Legazpi.

August

Davao holds the Kadayan sa Dabaw in August 16 to give thanks to the bountiful harvest of fruits and flowers. This is also the time when the waling-waling orchids are in full bloom. On the 28th day of August, Cagayan de Oro City celebrates the Feast Day of St. Augustine through their Kagay-An Festival.

September

The biggest celebration in the Bicol region is celebrated in September 19 through the Penafrancia Viva La Virgen feast where the patron saint is carried through the river with glowing floating candles. September 29 is the feast day of the patron saint of Iligan City, St. Michael the Archangel.

October

Bacolod City, Negros Occidental celebrates the Masskara Festival in October 18 with the purpose of urging locals to face and solve problems with a smiling face. From October 24 to 25, Camiguin Island celebrates the Lansones Festival in honor of their bountiful harvest of the lanzones fruit in the island.

November

In November, Angono, Rizal celebrates the Higantes Festival where gigantic paper mache puppets, as tall as 10 feet, are being carried by male devotees. This is celebrated from November 22 to 23.

December

The Giant Lantern Festival is celebrated in San Fernando, Pampanga on December 12. From December 9 to 21, Catholic devotees attend early morning masses for 9 days prior Christmas.

Travelers planning to visit the country will enjoy activities, festivals and events that are widely celebrated from one place to another. Every month holds a feast in different areas in the Philippines. That means that there is something new to look out for every month. Be sure to plan your visit and do a quick research with the festival that falls on your month of choice.

See You In The Philippines!

We hope you enjoyed this travel guide to the Philippines! After exploring all of the wonderful things the Philippines has to offer in this book, we hope that we have provided lots of inspiration as you plan your journey. Safe and happy travels, or as the Filipino's say, "Maligayang paglalakbáy"!

EXPERIENCE EVERYTHING TRAVEL GUIDE
COLLECTION™

EXPERIENCE
EVERYTHING
P U B L I S H I N G

www.ingramcontent.com/pod-product-compliance
Lightning Source LLC
Chambersburg PA
CBHW071740020426
42331CB00008B/2107